Acoustic Guitar Playing

Compiled and edited by
Tony Skinner and Laurence Harwood for

A CIP record for this publication is available from the British Library
ISBN: 978-1-905908-01-1

Printed and bound in Great Britain

Published by Registry Publications

Registry Mews, 11-13 Wilton Rd, Bexhill, Sussex, TN40 1HY

Compiled by

www.RGT.org

Acknowledgements
The editors are grateful for the advice and support of all members of the RGT's 'Acoustic Guitar Advisory Panel' during the compilation of this series, and in compiling this book are particularly indebted to Colin Berrido for his advice and contribution to the traditional melodies section.

Cover design and photography by JAK Images; back cover photographs courtesy of Moon Guitars and Freshman Guitars.
Page 22 photograph supplied by John Hornby Skewes Ltd.

v.20141103

CONTENTS

CD LISTING

INTRODUCTION

This publication is primarily intended for candidates considering taking the Registry of Guitar Tutors (RGT) Grade One examination in acoustic guitar playing. Those preparing for this examination should use this handbook in conjunction with the Acoustic Guitar Exam Information Booklet and Acoustic Guitar syllabus – both freely downloadable from the RGT website: www.RGT.org

PERFORMANCE AWARDS

This handbook can also be used for the RGT Level One Performance Award in Acoustic Guitar Playing. The Performance Award focuses entirely on the performance of three pieces: one Rhythm Playing Study, one Fingerstyle Study and one melody chosen from this handbook. Performance Awards enable candidates to submit a video or audio recording and have it professionally assessed, and so are very useful for candidates who prefer not to attend an examination centre.

Go to www.RGT.org for more information.

NOTATION

In order that chords and scales can be made available for all to understand regardless of experience, they are illustrated in three formats: traditional notation, tablature and fretboxes – thereby ensuring that there is no doubt as to what is required. Each of these methods of notation is explained below.

TABLATURE

Horizontal lines represent the strings (with the top line being the high E string). The numbers on the string lines refer to the frets. **0** on a line means play that string open (unfretted). The example below means play at the second fret on the third string.

MUSICAL NOTATION

Each line, and space between lines, represents a different note. Leger lines are used to extend the stave for low or high notes.

For scales at this grade, string and fret numbers are printed below the notation. Fret-hand fingering is shown with the numbers **1 2 3 4**, with **0** indicating an open string. String numbers are shown in a circle.

The example below shows the C major scale.

FRETBOXES

Vertical lines represent the strings – with the line furthest to the right representing the high E string.

Horizontal lines represent the frets.

The numbers on the lines show the recommended fingering. (**1** represents the index finger, **2** = the long middle finger, **3** = the ring finger, **4** = the little finger.)

This example means play with the second finger at the second fret on the G string.

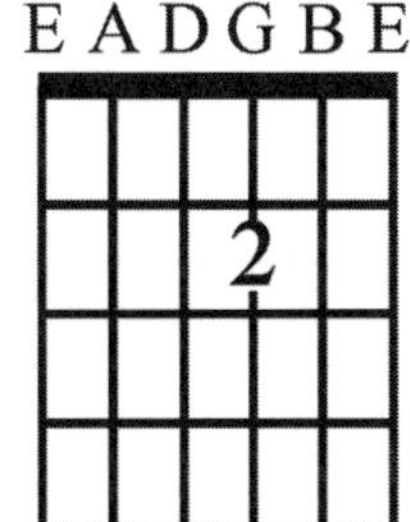

FINGERING OPTIONS

The fingerings (including tablature positions) that have been chosen are those that are most likely to be effective for the widest range of players at this level. However, there is a variety of alternative fingerings that could be used, and any systematic and effective fingerings that produce a good musical result will be acceptable; there is no requirement to use the exact fingerings shown within this handbook. Throughout the examination, it is entirely the candidate's choice as to whether a pick (plectrum) or fingers are used to pick the strings. A thumbpick can be used if desired.

CD

A CD is supplied with this handbook as a learning aid and the recorded performances are designed specifically to provide an indication of the standard of playing expected at this grade.

TUNING

The use of an electronic tuner or other tuning aid, prior to or at the start of the examination, is permitted; candidates should be able to make any further adjustments, if required during the examination, unaided. The examiner will, upon request, offer an E or A note to tune to.

For examination purposes guitars should be tuned to Standard Concert Pitch (A=440Hz). A tuning guide is provided on the accompanying CD on Track 1.

EXAMINATION ENTRY

An examination entry form is provided at the back of this handbook. This is the only valid entry form for the RGT acoustic guitar examinations.

Please note that *if the entry form is detached and lost, it will not be replaced under any circumstances* and the candidate will be required to obtain a replacement handbook to obtain another entry form.

The entry form includes a unique entry code to enable you to enter online via the RGT website **www.RGT.org**

FINGERBOARD KNOWLEDGE

The examiner will choose a selection of the chords and scales shown in this chapter and ask the candidate to play them *from memory*. In addition, the examiner may ask the candidate to play any of the chords or scales from Preliminary Grade:

- Open position chords: G, C, D, Am, Dm, Em
- One octave open position major scales: C, G

(Candidates should refer to the Preliminary Grade handbook if they are not familiar with any of these chords or scales, particularly as these will be used within the Performance, Accompaniment and Aural Assessment sections of the examination.)

Chords and scales can be played using either the fingers or a pick (plectrum). Overall, the examiner will be listening for accurate, clear and even playing. Prompt presentations, without undue delay or hesitation after being asked to play a chord or scale, will be taken as an indication of secure knowledge.

Pressing with the tips of the fingers, as close to the fretwire as possible, will aid clarity. This technique will help eliminate fretbuzz and minimise the amount of fretting pressure required – enabling you to play with a lighter, clearer and therefore more fluent touch.

A maximum of 10 marks may be awarded in this section of the examination.

CHORDS

Chords should be played using a single slow strum, starting with the lowest (root) note. The whole chord shape should be carefully placed on the fingerboard before, and kept on during, playing.

Ensure that no required open strings are muted (these are marked with a **0** by the fretbox).

A string which should be omitted when playing a chord is marked with an **X** by the fretbox, so be very careful not to strike this string when playing the chord.

CHORD SYMBOLS

This handbook (and examination) use the following standard abbreviations when referring to chords:

- The symbol for a major chord is the capital letter of the name of the chord. For example, the symbol for E major is **E**.
- The symbol for a minor chord is the capital letter of the name of the chord plus lower case **m**. For example, the symbol for E minor is **Em.**
- The symbol for a dominant seventh chord is the capital letter of the name of the chord followed by the number 7. For example, the symbol for E dominant 7 is **E7.**

A major

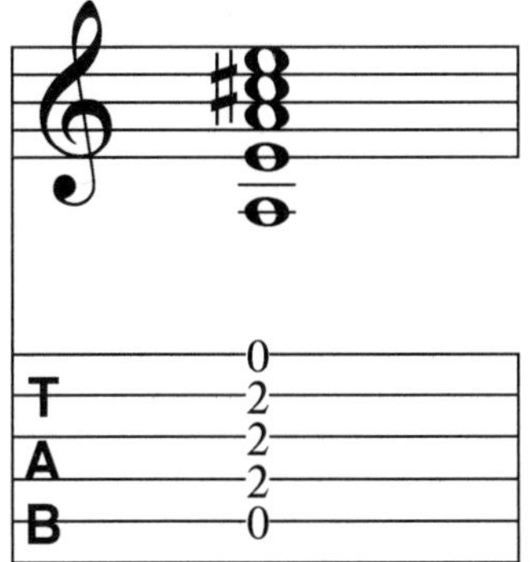

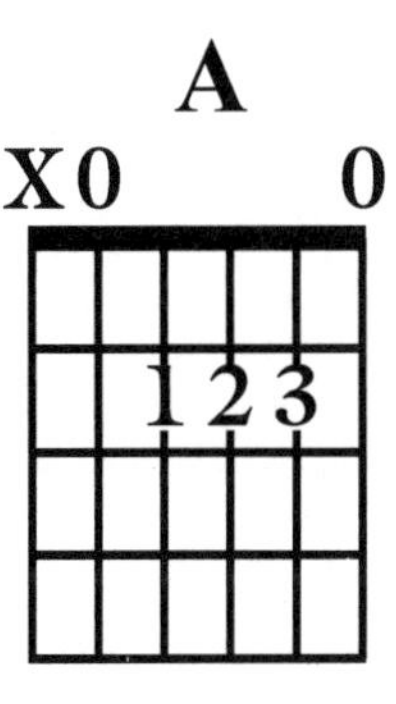

E major

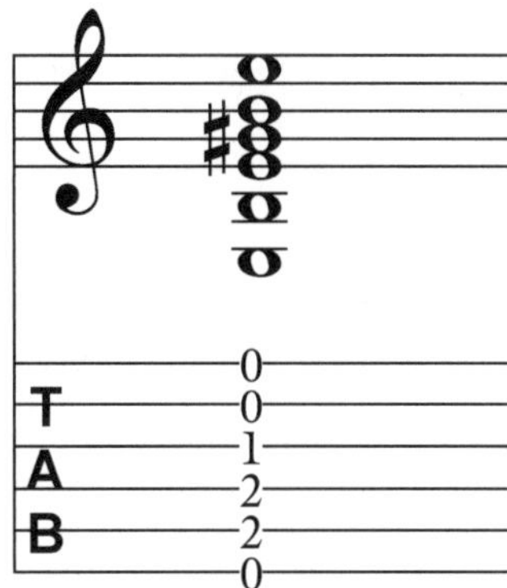

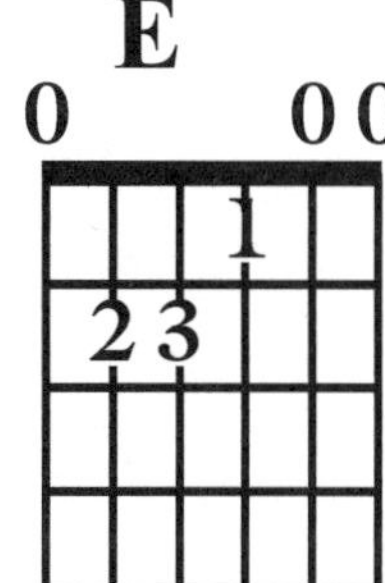

A dominant 7

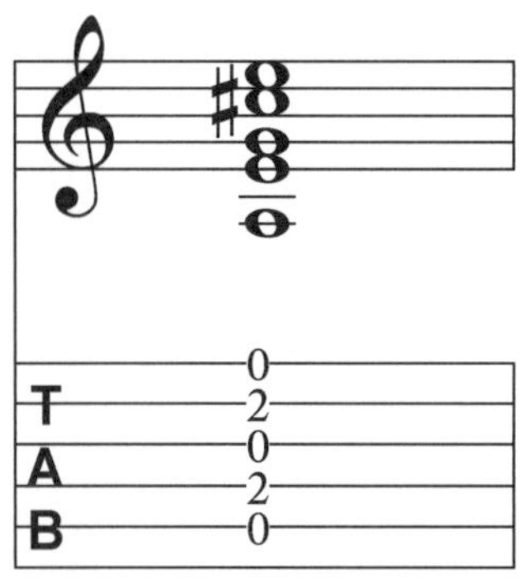

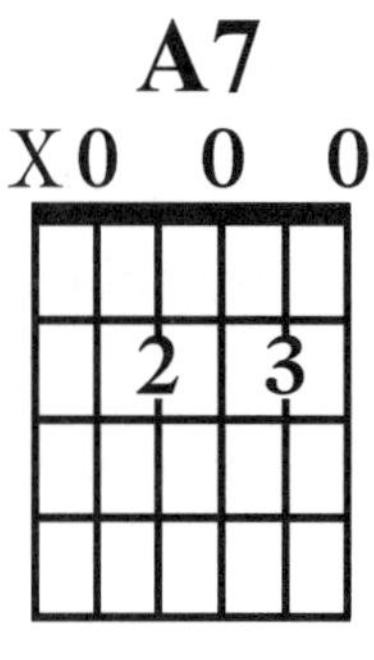

B dominant 7

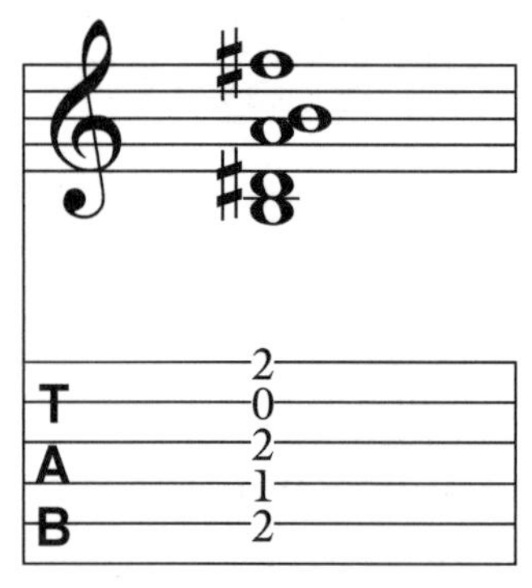

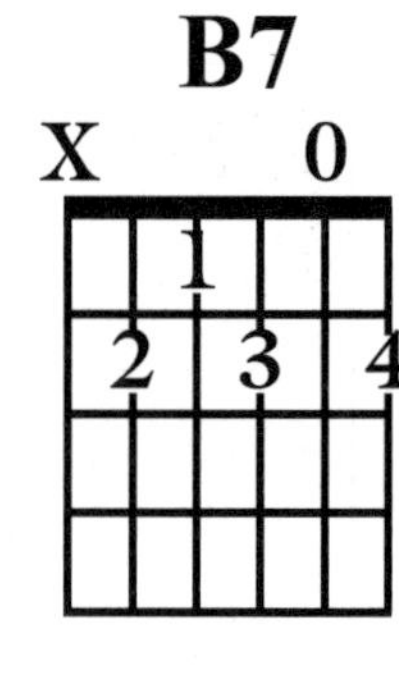

D dominant 7

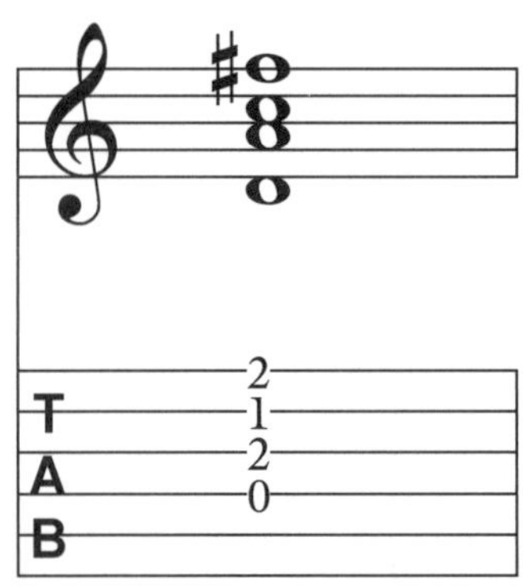

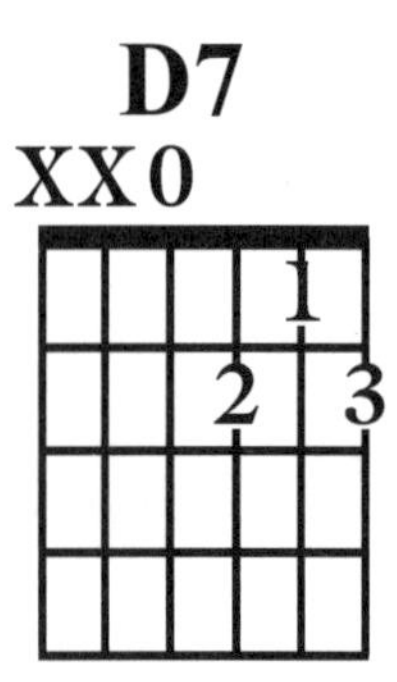

E dominant 7

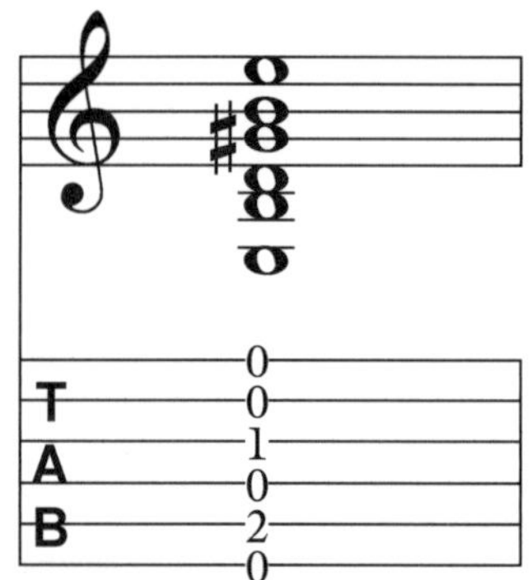

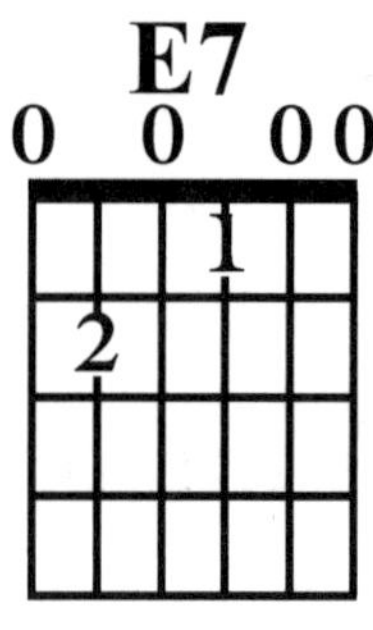

CHORD SUMMARY

The chords required for Grade One are:
A, E, A7, B7, D7, E7
plus, from Preliminary Grade:
G, C, D, Am, Dm, Em

LISTEN AND LEARN
All of the set chords can be heard on CD track 2

SCALES

Scales should be played ascending and descending, i.e. from the lowest note to the highest and back again without repeating, or pausing at, the top note. Scales should be played at an approximate tempo of 108 beats per minute. (This suggested tempo is for general guidance only and slightly slower or faster performances will be acceptable, providing that the tempo is maintained evenly throughout.)

D major scale – 1 octave

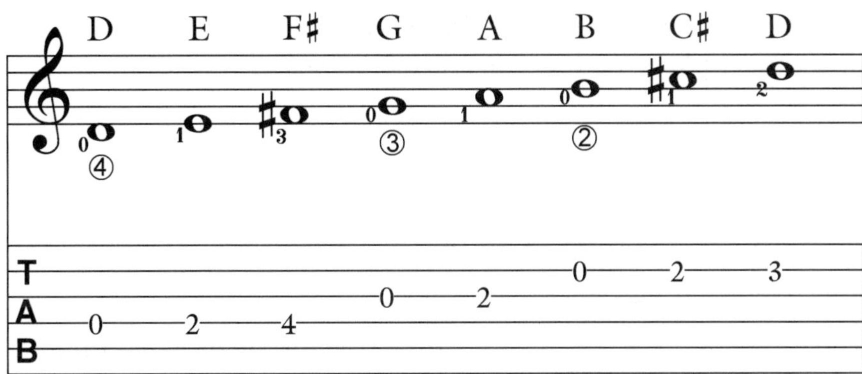

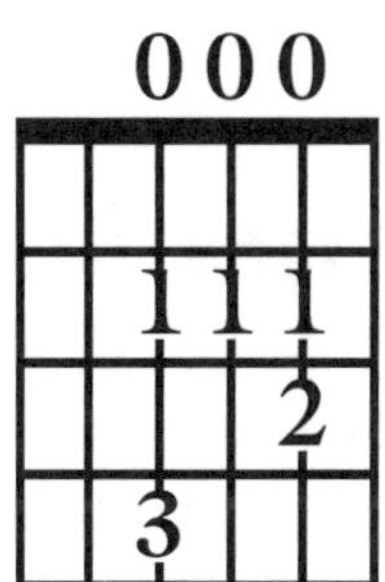

A natural minor scale – 1 octave

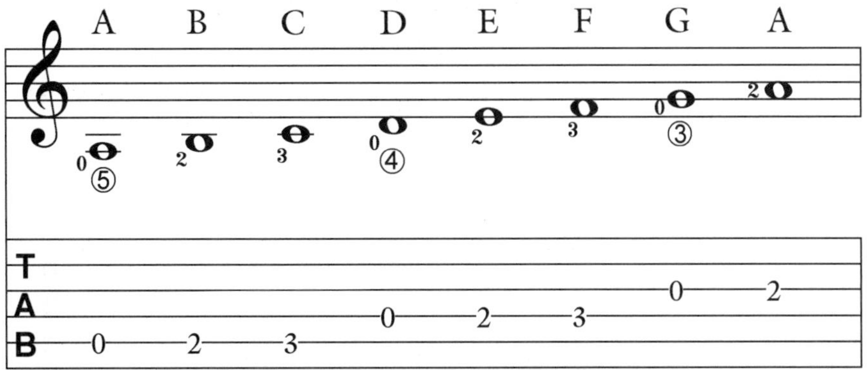

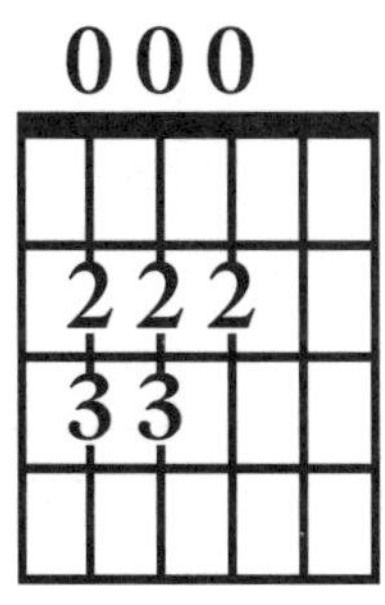

SCALE SUMMARY

The scales required for Grade One are:
D major and A natural minor
plus, from Preliminary Grade:
C major and G major

LISTEN AND LEARN
All of the set scales can be heard on CD track 3

PERFORMANCE

Candidates should select and play a total of TWO pieces comprised of ONE Rhythm Playing Study plus *either* ONE Fingerstyle Study *or* ONE melody.

Performances do not need to be from memory: the handbook may be used during this section of the exam. Candidates should remember to bring the handbook to the exam if they do not intend to play from memory; photocopies will not be permitted.

RHYTHM PLAYING STUDIES

The candidate must select and perform, using the prescribed strum pattern, ONE of the Rhythm Playing Studies in this chapter.

- Each study consists of an 8-bar chord progression that is played twice before ending on the key chord.
- After the repeat section, the final closing bar should be played with just a single strum.
- Tempo indications are for general guidance only.
- A pick (plectrum) is recommended but fingers, or fingers and a pick, can be used if preferred.
- It is recommended that you start each bar with a downstroke strum, but the use of downstrums and upstrums is left entirely to the candidate's discretion: any combination is acceptable providing a good musical result is achieved.

RHYTHM PLAYING ADVICE

A maximum of 25 marks may be awarded for the Rhythm Playing Study.

In order to achieve the most musical performance and obtain a high mark in the exam, you should aim for the following when performing the Rhythm Playing Study:

- A secure knowledge of the chord shapes and the facility to change from one chord shape to another smoothly and without hesitation or delay.
- Clear sounding chords that are free of fretbuzz and any unintended muting of notes. Pressing with the tips of the fretting fingers, as close as possible to the fretwire, will help achieve this.
- A flowing rhythm style, maintaining an even tempo throughout.
- Accurate reproduction of the notated strum pattern.

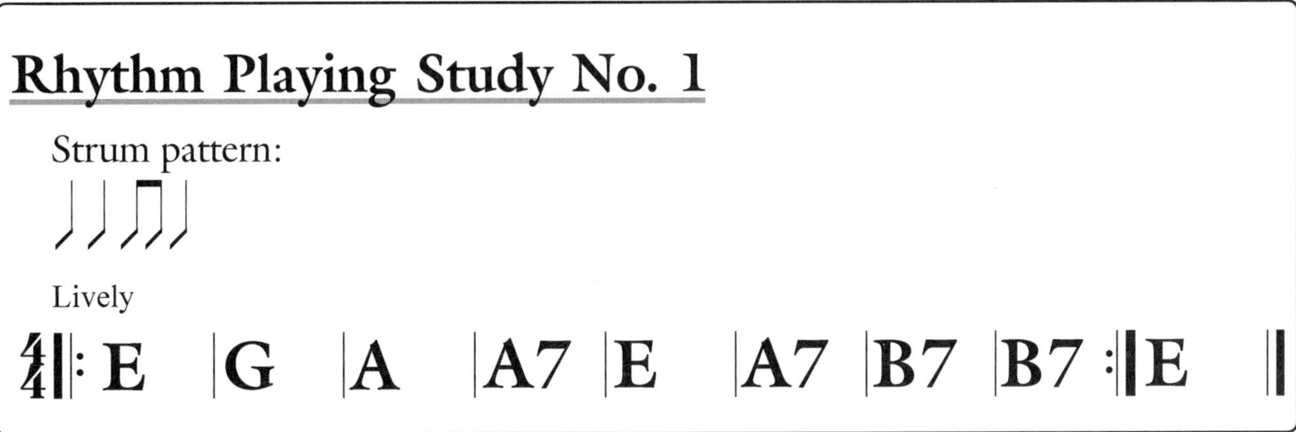

This study is in $\frac{4}{4}$ time – meaning that there are four main beats per bar.

The notated strum pattern indicates that you should play on all four beats, with an extra strum inserted between beats 3 and 4: **1 2 3&4**

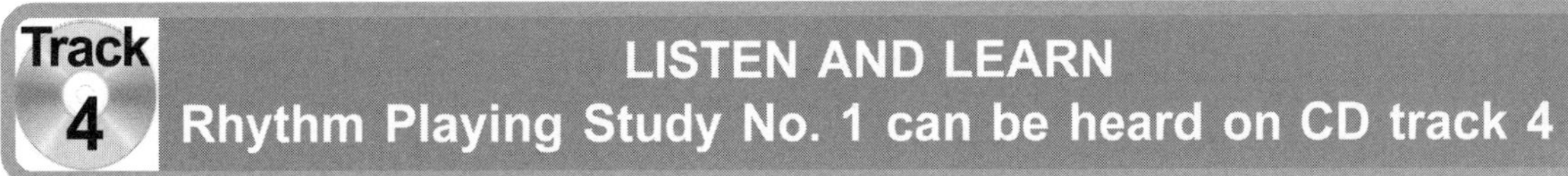

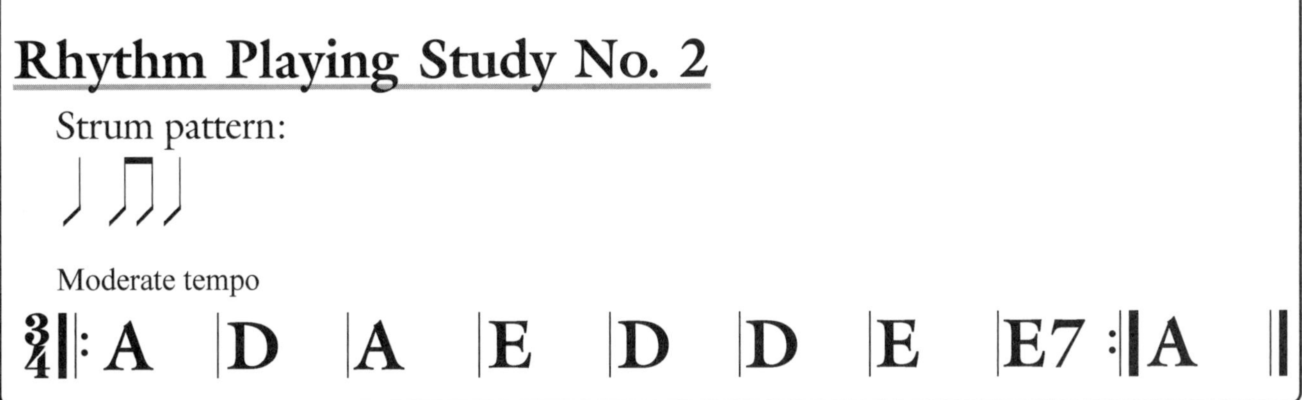

This study is in $\frac{3}{4}$ time – meaning that there are three main beats per bar.

The notated strum pattern indicates that you should play on all 3 beats, with an extra strum inserted between beats 2 and 3: **1 2&3**

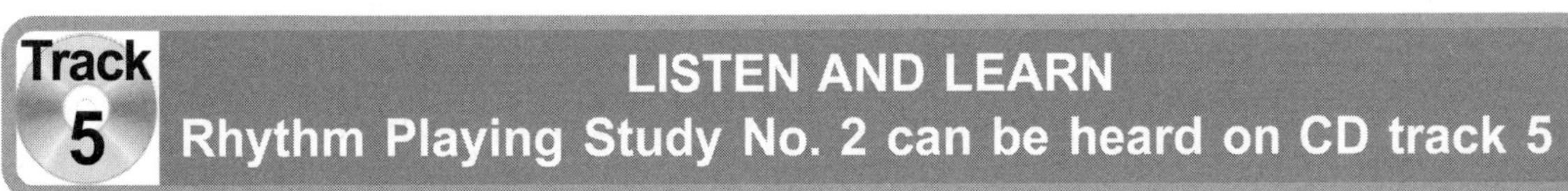

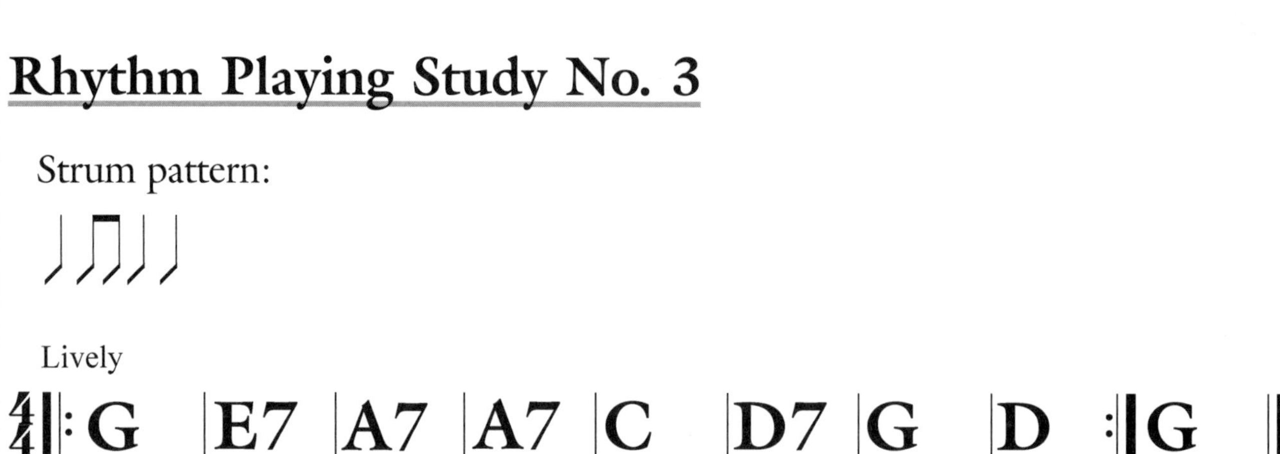

This study is in $\frac{4}{4}$ time – meaning that there are four main beats per bar. The notated strum pattern ♩♫♩♩ indicates that you should play on all four beats, with an extra strum inserted between beats 2 and 3: **1 2&3 4**

Track 6

LISTEN AND LEARN

Rhythm Playing Study No. 3 can be heard on CD track 6

Candidates can choose to play *either*: one of the following Fingerstyle Studies, OR a melody from the next section in this chapter.

FINGERSTYLE STUDIES

- Each fingerstyle study consists of an 8-bar notated chord progression that incorporates a common fingerstyle pattern.
- The study should be played twice before ending on the key chord.
- Tempo indications are for general guidance only.
- Chord symbols are provided as an aid to study and performance. It is recommended that you finger the entire chord shape even if certain strings are not intended to be used: this has the benefit that if you accidentally strike an unrequired string it may still fit with the other notes being played.
- Pick-hand fingering is indicated as follows: **p** = thumb, **i** = index finger, **m** = middle finger, **a** = third finger. The pick-hand fingering shown on the notation is recommended as it is likely to be the most effective for the widest range of players at this level, however there is a variety of alternative fingerings that could be used and any systematic and effective fingerings that produce a good musical result will be acceptable.

FINGERSTYLE ADVICE

A maximum of 25 marks may be awarded for the Fingerstyle Study.

In order to achieve the most musical performance and obtain a high mark in the exam, you should aim for the following when performing the Fingerstyle Study:

- Accurate reproduction of the notated fingerstyle pattern.
- Secure knowledge of the chord shapes used and the ability to keep all the required notes sounding clearly.
- A fluent picking style, maintaining an even tempo throughout.
- The ability to change smoothly from one chord shape to another without cutting off notes from the previous bar early.

Fingerstyle Study No. 1

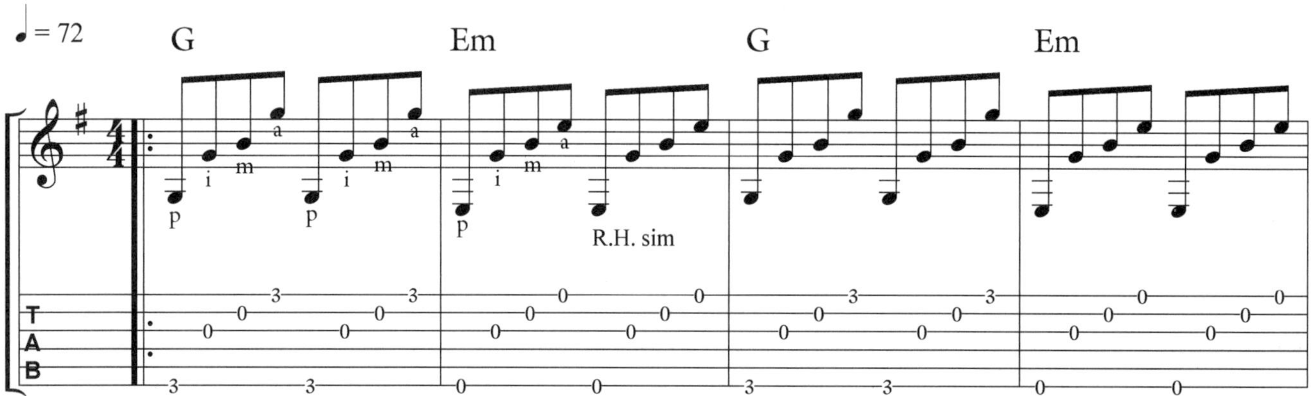

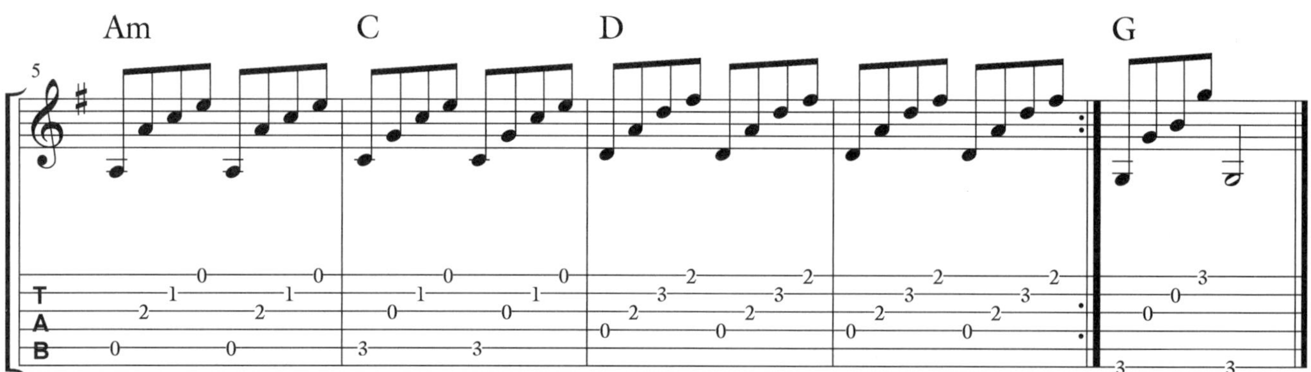

This study uses the fingering pattern **pima** throughout. This means that you should start with the thumb playing the bass note, the treble strings are then picked from the third string to the first string using the first, second and third fingers respectively.

LISTEN AND LEARN
Fingerstyle Study No. 1 can be heard on CD track 7

Fingerstyle Study No. 2

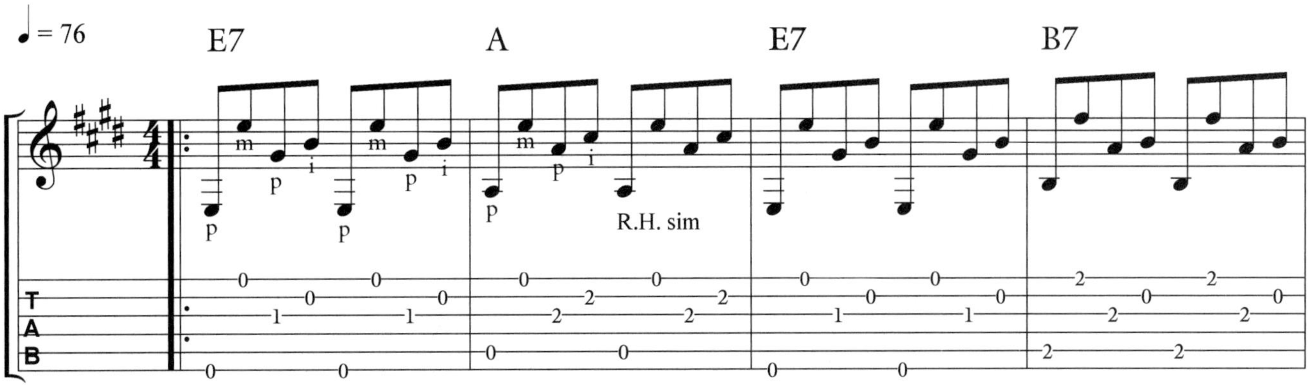

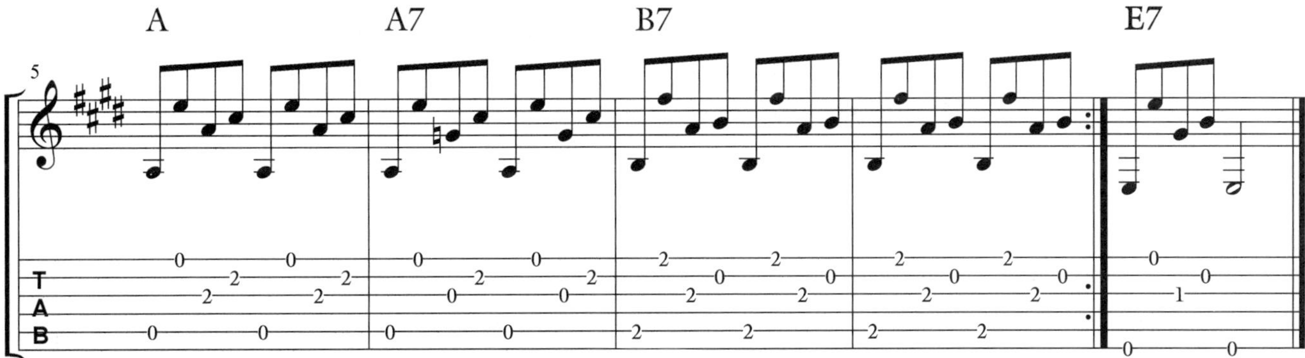

This study uses the fingering pattern **pmpi** throughout. This means that you should start with the thumb playing the bass note, the top string is then picked with the middle finger, the thumb then picks the third string, followed by the first finger picking the second string. This style is sometimes called 'double thumb pick' because the thumb is used twice within each bar.

Track 8

LISTEN AND LEARN

Fingerstyle Study No. 2 can be heard on CD track 8

MELODIES

If not performing a fingerstyle study, candidates can instead select and perform ONE of the four traditional melodies that follow in this chapter or, if preferred, the melody can be a 'free choice' by the candidate of any other well-known melody from 1960 onwards – providing it is of at least similar technical standard and duration to the melodies below. (Whenever possible, candidates should bring the notation of the free choice melody to the exam for the examiner to view.) Melodies can be played with a pick or using fingers, as preferred by the candidate.

Chord symbols are provided for each melody purely to enable a teacher or fellow player to provide accompaniment during practice. Candidates are NOT required to play the chords in the exam – only the melody, unaccompanied. (On the CD an accompaniment is played with the melody to enhance the musical effect and reinforce the timing for learning purposes.)

Tempo markings have been chosen that reflect the capabilities expected at this level, but are for general guidance only: faster, or slightly slower, tempos can be used providing they produce an effective musical result.

MELODY PLAYING ADVICE

A maximum of 25 marks may be awarded in the melody playing section of the exam.

As the melodies are based on the scales set for the Fingerboard Knowledge section of the exam (including the C and G major scales from Preliminary Grade), practising these scales will make learning the melodies much easier.

In order to achieve the most musical performance and obtain a high mark in the exam you should aim for the following when performing the melodies:

- An accurate reproduction of the pitch and rhythm of the melody.
- A fluent rendition, maintaining an even tempo throughout.
- Capturing the phrasing within the melody.
- Clear sounding notes that are free of fretbuzz.

Auld Lang Syne

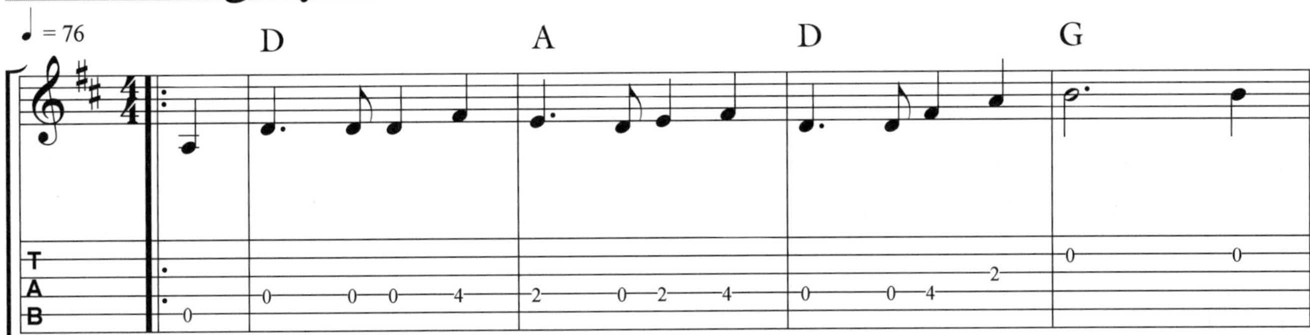

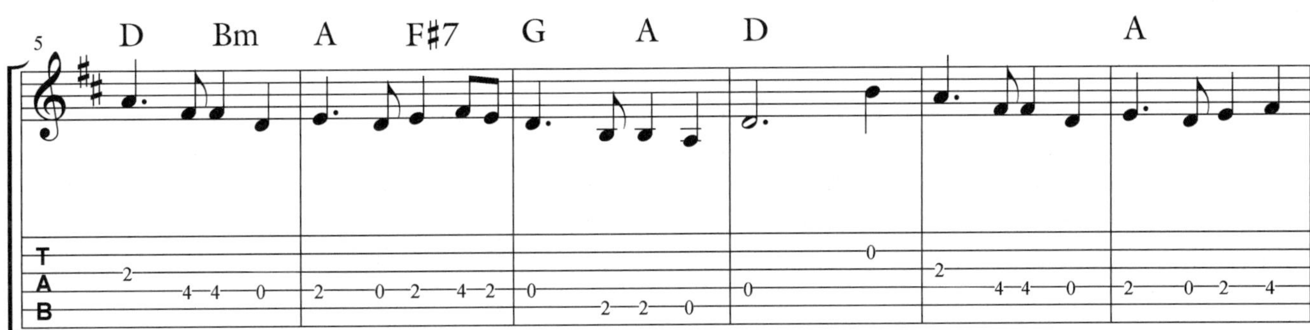

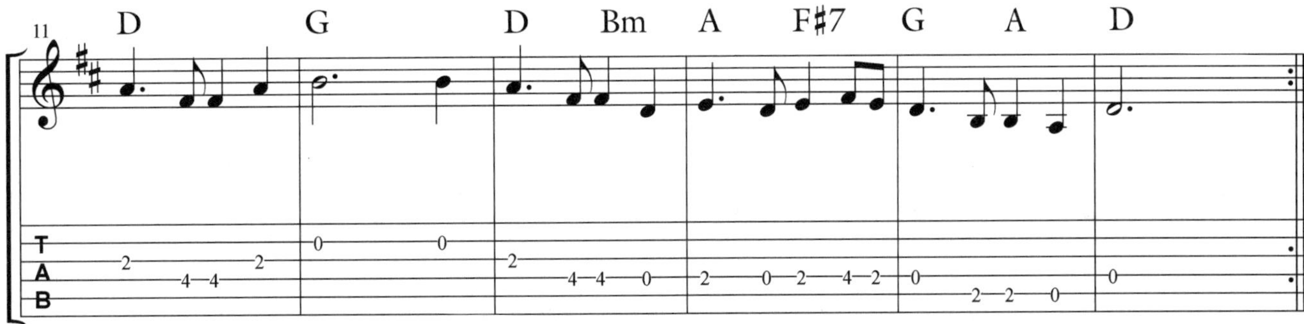

This melody is in $\frac{4}{4}$ time and is made up of four phrases that are almost identical rhythmically. Notice how the melody starts with a bar containing just one note – this is known as a 'pickup' or 'anacrusis'. Another rhythmic feature of this melody is the dotted rhythm at the start of many bars.

The melody is notated in the key of D major.

Chord symbols are provided purely to enable a teacher or fellow player to provide accompaniment during practice. Candidates are NOT expected to play these chords in this section of the exam.

Track 9

LISTEN AND LEARN
Auld Lang Syne can be heard on CD track 9

The Bear Dance

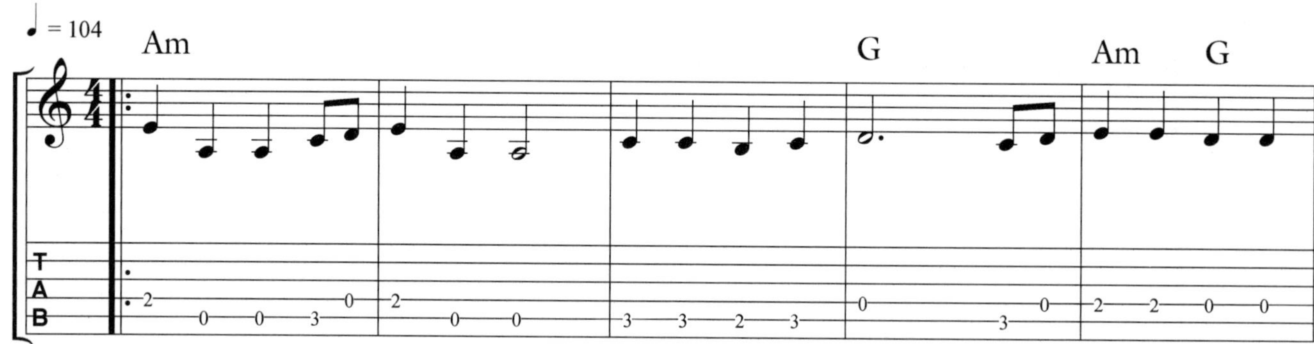

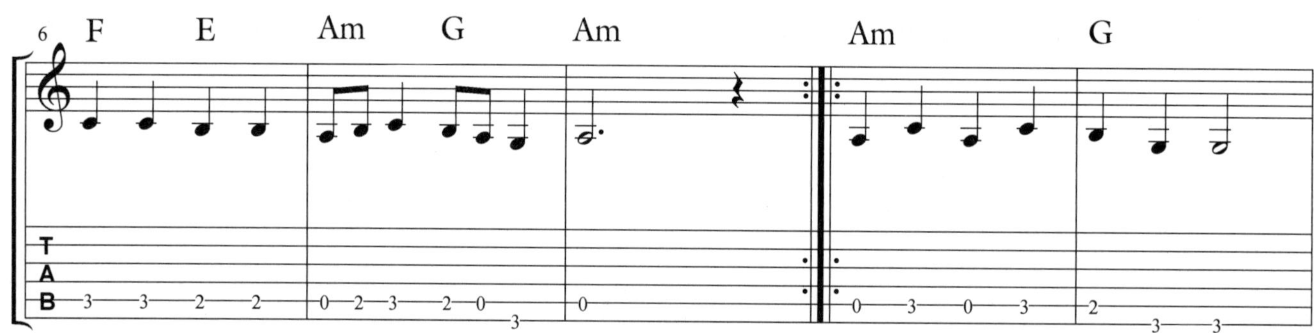

This melody is in $\frac{4}{4}$ time. It is in two 8-bar sections, both of which are repeated. The last five bars of each section are identical.

The melody is notated in the key of A minor. It should be played at quite a lively tempo in order to capture the 'dance' feel of the music.

LISTEN AND LEARN

The Bear Dance can be heard on CD track 10

Mairi's Wedding

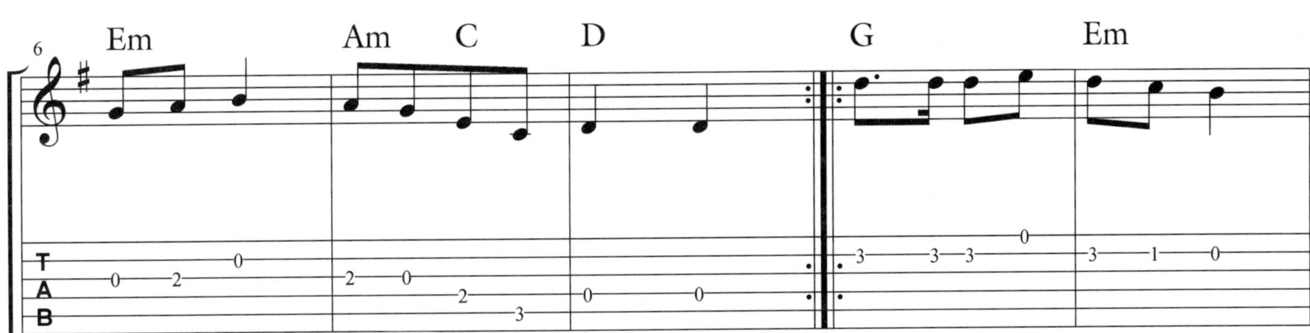

This melody is in $\frac{2}{4}$ time and is notated in the key of G major. It is in two 8-bar sections, both of which are repeated. Notice how the second section (from bar 9 onwards) is rhythmically identical to the first, even though some of the notes are different. Watch out for the dotted rhythm that appears at the start of every four bar phrase.

LISTEN AND LEARN

Mairi's Wedding can be heard on CD track 11

Swing Low Sweet Chariot

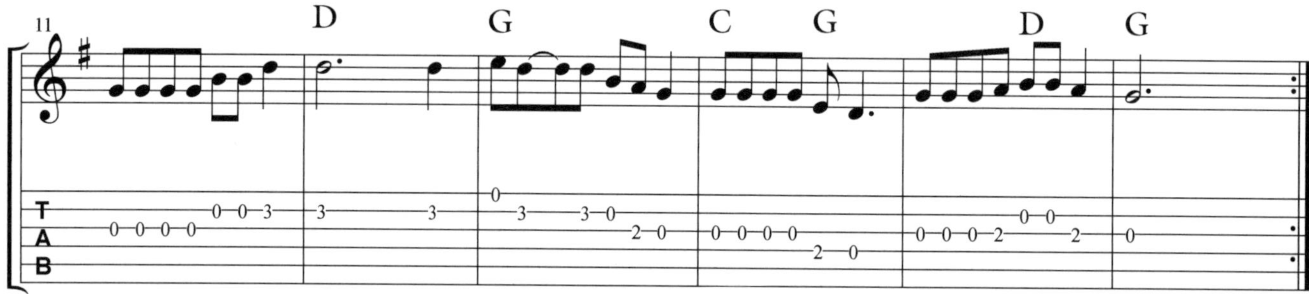

This melody is in $\frac{4}{4}$ time and is notated in the key of G major.

Notice how the dotted rhythm and notes in bar 2 are repeated in bar 6. The distinctive eighth note rhythm in bar 3 is repeated in bars 7, 11 and 15.

Track 12

LISTEN AND LEARN
Swing Low Sweet Chariot can be heard on CD track 12

MUSICAL KNOWLEDGE

The examiner will ask a range of questions, from the topics listed below, to test the candidate's knowledge about the basic anatomy of the guitar.

NOTES ON THE FINGERBOARD

Candidates may be asked to name any note taken from the scales set for this and previous grades. A summary of these is given below.

Fret

String	0	1	2	3	4
1	E	(F)	F♯(G♭)	G	(G♯/ A♭)
2	B	C	C♯(D♭)	D	(D♯/ E♭)
3	G	(G♯/ A♭)	A	(A♯/ B♭)	(B)
4	D	(D♯/ E♭)	E	F	F♯(G♭)
5	A	(A♯/ B♭)	B	C	(C♯/ D♭)
6	(E)	(F)	(F♯ / G♭)	(G)	(G♯/ A♭)

The notes shown in brackets do not occur in any of the set scales for this and previous grades, and are provided here only for completeness; knowledge of these will not be tested in the exam.

PARTS OF THE GUITAR

Candidates should be able to demonstrate a basic knowledge of the anatomy of the acoustic guitar by being able to identify the location of the parts of the guitar shown on the illustration overleaf:

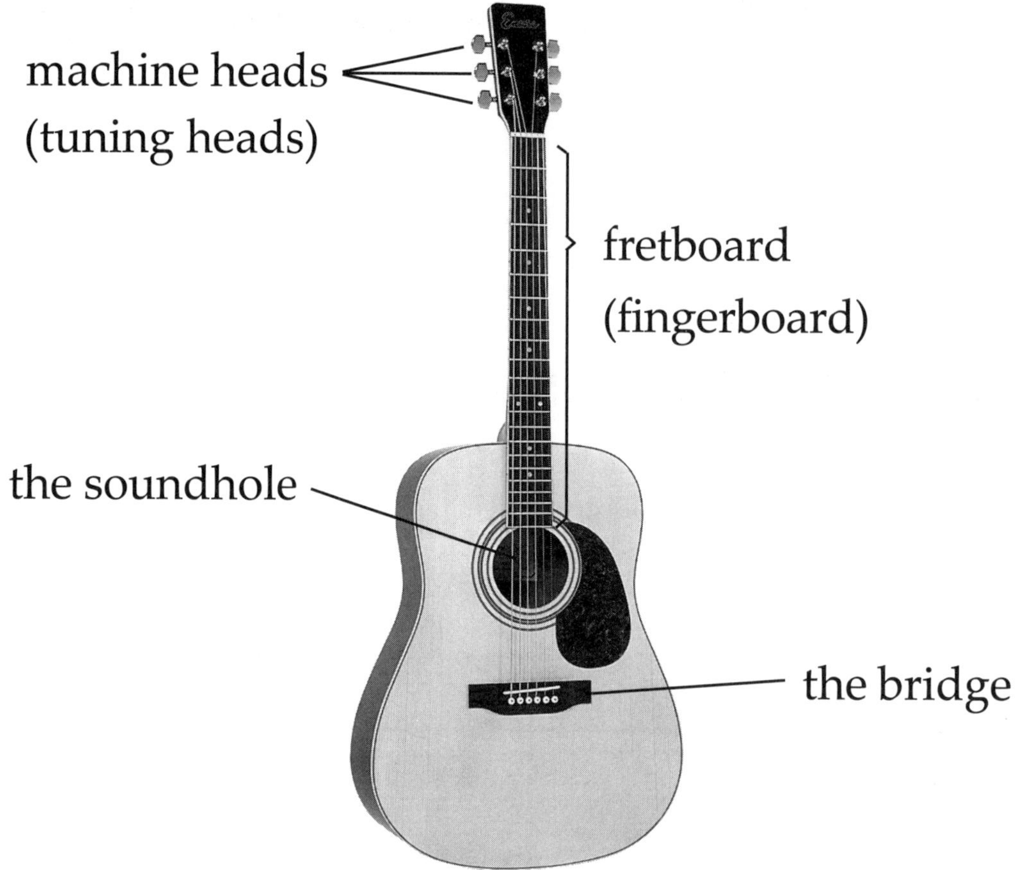

MUSICAL KNOWLEDGE ADVICE

A maximum of 10 marks may be awarded in this section of the exam.

Knowing the names of the notes on the fingerboard helps to provide a secure musical foundation. Knowledge of the names of the main parts of the guitar will also prove useful when communicating with other guitarists. Being able to demonstrate secure knowledge in all of these areas will help you gain a high mark in this section of the exam.

In order to gain the highest marks, responses to the examiner's questions should be prompt and confident – demonstrating that the answers are known, rather than guessed or worked out.

ACCOMPANIMENT

In this section of the exam, the candidate should play a chordal accompaniment while the examiner plays an eight-bar riff-based melody (either live on guitar or keyboard, or via a recording).

- The candidate will be shown a chord chart for the melody. The examiner will then give a one bar count-in and play the melody once for the candidate to listen to without playing along.

- The examiner will then give another one bar count-in and the melody will be played a further three times without stopping. The candidate can accompany the first of these three verses if they wish to, but only the accompaniment of the second and third verses will be assessed.

It is recommended that during the first (unassessed) accompaniment verse a chord is strummed on the first beat of each bar so that the timing can be established. Alternatively, the candidate may prefer just to read through the chord chart and listen as the examiner plays the first verse of melody.

At this grade, there will be three different chords in the accompaniment chord chart. The range of chords will be restricted to the chords required for this and previous grades. There will be two bars of each chord, apart from the very final bar (after the repeat), in which the final chord should be played with a single strum. The time signature will be $\frac{4}{4}$.

The style of the accompaniment is left to the candidate's discretion, and the candidate can chose to either strum or fingerpick. The CD recording that comes with this book provides an indication of the technical level that would be expected for a high mark at this grade – only the two assessed verses are provided for each example. It is NOT intended that candidates copy the style of accompaniments performed on the CD recording – these are provided purely as examples of the standard required – and candidates are strongly encouraged to devise their own rhythmic/picking styles; these should always relate to the style and timing of the melody played by the examiner.

The melody notation played by the examiner will not be seen by the candidate.

ACCOMPANIMENT ADVICE

A maximum of 20 marks may be awarded in this section of the exam.

In order to achieve the most musical performance and obtain a high mark in the exam you should aim for the following when performing your accompaniment:

- Remember that the very first time the examiner plays the melody, you have the chance to listen to it without needing to play along. Use this opportunity to listen carefully and try to absorb the melodic shape and structure of the melody.
- In the first verse of the three continuous playings your playing will not be assessed, so you can best use this time by reading through the chord chart and just strumming once on the first beat of each bar so that the timing becomes clearly fixed in your mind.
- In the remaining two verses use an appropriate rhythm or picking style that suits the mood, style and timing of the melody.
- Keep listening to the melody while playing your accompaniment and make sure to keep in time with it. Use your knowledge of the chord shapes to change smoothly from one chord to another, whilst making sure your chords ring clear.
- Try to include some variation in the final verse.

Two examples of the *type* of test that will occur are given on the following pages. Note that each of the Accompaniment Examples is provided only as a sample of the *type* of melody and chord symbols that may occur in the exam.

MORE ACCOMPANIMENT PRACTICE

A supplementary book/CD is available to provide you with extra practice and advice for this section of the exam.

See inside back cover of this handbook for more information.

Accompaniment Example 1

Chord chart

4/4 ‖: Am	Am	Em	Em

Am	Am	G	G	:‖ Am ‖

Melody

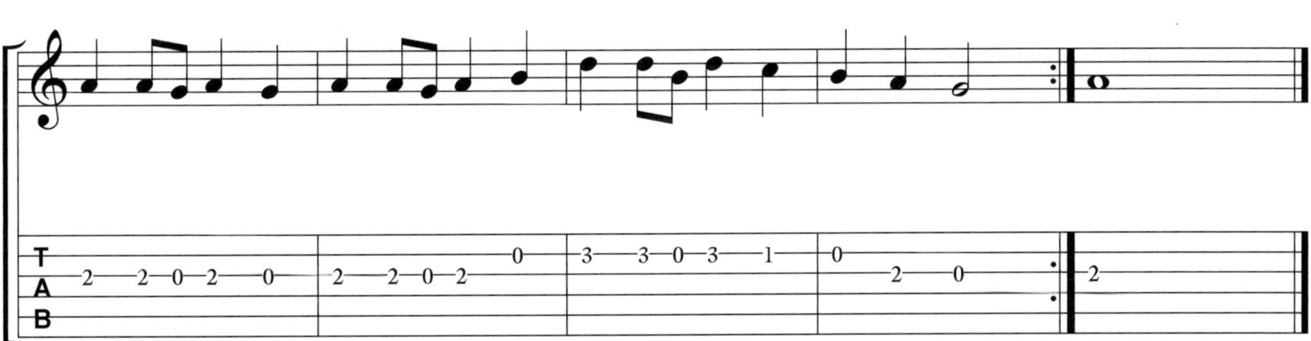

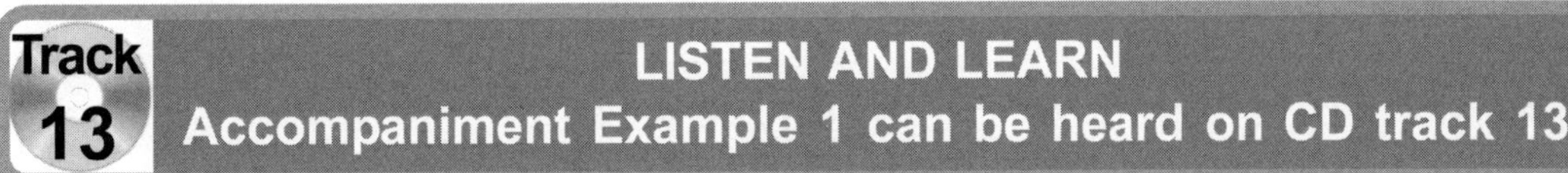

Accompaniment Example 2

Chord chart

| 4/4 ‖: D | D | A7 | A7 |

| G | G | A7 | A7 | :‖ D ‖

Melody

LISTEN AND LEARN
Accompaniment Example 2 can be heard on CD track 14

AURAL ASSESSMENT

The candidate will be given a selection of rhythm, pitch and harmony tests. The examiner will play these either on guitar or keyboard (live or via a recording). Examples of the tests are provided below; these are also included on the accompanying CD.

A maximum of 10 marks may be awarded in total during this section of the examination.

RHYTHM TESTS

The examiner will twice play a four bar melody in either $\frac{3}{4}$ or $\frac{4}{4}$ time. The rhythm will consist of a mixture of half notes (minims), quarter notes (crotchets) and eighth notes (quavers).

Test a) During the second playing the candidate should clap or tap the main pulse, accenting the first beat of each bar.

Test b) The candidate should then identify the time signature as either $\frac{3}{4}$ or $\frac{4}{4}$ time.

Test c) The examiner will play any ONE bar of the melody twice. The candidate should reproduce the exact rhythm by clapping or tapping.

Three examples demonstrating the *type* of rhythm tests that will occur at this grade are shown below.

Example 1 (CD track 15)

Example 2 (CD track 16)

Example 3 (CD track 17)

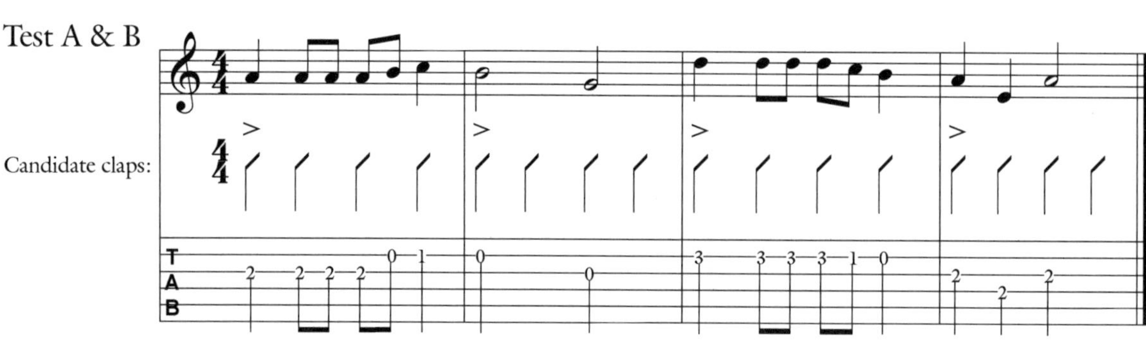

PITCH AND HARMONY TESTS

Test d) The candidate should look away while the examiner plays a five-note phrase consisting of *adjacent* notes taken from the C major scale. The phrase will start on the keynote. The examiner will play the phrase twice before the candidate makes a first attempt to reproduce the phrase on the guitar. If required, the candidate can request the examiner to play the phrase one further time, prior to the candidate's second attempt. However, the candidate will then be expected to reproduce the phrase promptly and will not be permitted any further attempts at 'working it out'. Some examples of the *type* of phrase are shown below. These can be heard on CD track 18.

Example 1

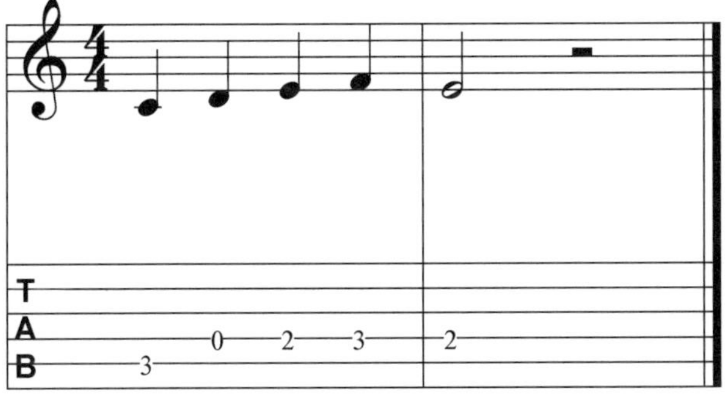

Example 2

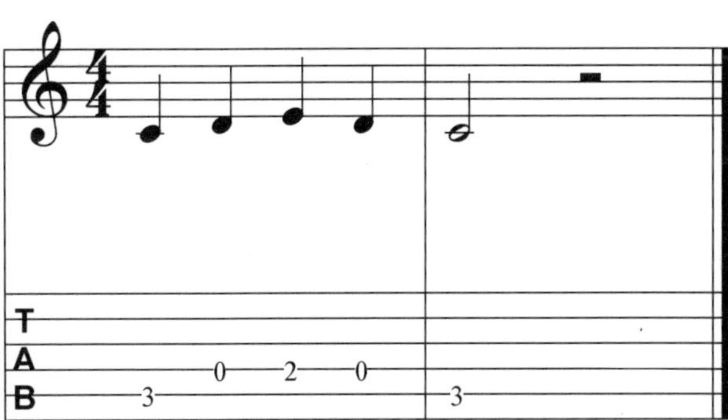

Example 3

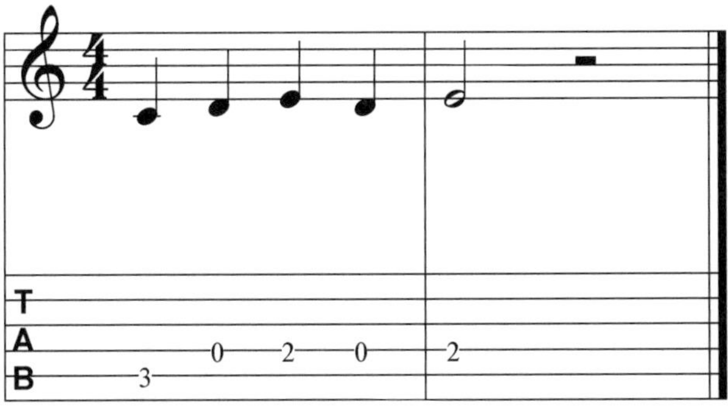

Example 4

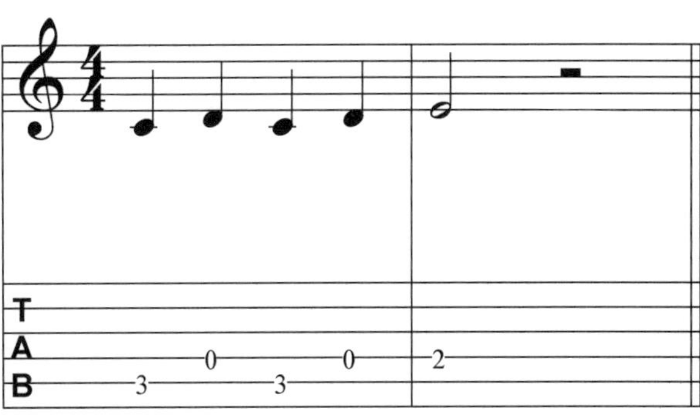

Test e) The candidate should look away while the examiner plays a short chord progression containing either all major chords, all minor chords or all dominant seventh chords. The candidate will then be asked to state whether the progression consisted of major, minor or dominant seventh chords. Below are some examples of the style of test:

Example 1 (CD track 19)

3/4 || **A** | **D** | **E** | **A** || = major

Example 2 (CD track 20)

3/4 || **Am** | **Dm** | **Em** | **Am** || = minor

Example 3 (CD track 21)

3/4 || **A7** | **D7** | **E7** | **A7** || = dominant seventh

Examination Entry Form

Acoustic Guitar | Grade 1

ONLINE ENTRY – AVAILABLE FOR UK CANDIDATES ONLY

For **UK candidates**, entries and payments can be made online at www.RGT.org, using the entry code below. You will be able to pay the entry fee by credit or debit card at a secure payment page on the website.

Your exam entry code is: **AA-6461-XN**

Once you have entered online, you should sign this form overleaf. **You must bring this signed form to your exam and hand it to the examiner in order to be admitted to the exam room.**

If NOT entering online, please complete BOTH sides of this form and return to the address overleaf.

SESSION (Spring/Summer/Winter): ____________________ YEAR: ___________

Dates/times NOT available: ____

Note: Only name specific dates (and times on those dates) when it would be absolutely impossible for you to attend due to important prior commitments (such as pre-booked overseas travel) which cannot be cancelled. We will then endeavour to avoid scheduling an exam session in your area on those dates. In fairness to all other candidates in your area, only list dates on which it would be impossible for you to attend. An entry form that blocks out unreasonable periods may be returned. (Exams may be held on any day of the week including, but not exclusively, weekends. Exams may be held within or outside of the school term.)

Candidate Details: *Please write as clearly as possible using BLOCK CAPITALS*

Candidate Name (as to appear on certificate): ______________________________

Address: ____

____ Postcode: ___________________

Tel. No. (day): ___________________________ (mobile): ________________________

IMPORTANT: Take care to write your email address below as clearly as possible, as your exam entry acknowledgement and your exam appointment details will be sent to this email address. Only provide an email address that is in regular monitored use.

Email: ____

Where an email address is provided your exam correspondence will be sent by email only, and not by post. This will ensure your exam correspondence will reach you sooner.

Teacher Details *(if applicable)*

Teacher Name (as to appear on certificate): ______________________________

RGT Tutor Code (if applicable): __________________

Address: ____

____ Postcode: ___________________

Tel. No. (day): ___________________________ (mobile): ________________________

Email: ____

RGT Acoustic Guitar Official Entry Form

The standard LCM entry form is NOT valid for RGT exam entries.
Entry to the exam is only possible via this original form.
Photocopies of this form will not be accepted under any circumstances.

- Completion of this entry form is an agreement to comply with the current syllabus requirements and conditions of entry published at www.RGT.org. Where candidates are entered for exams by a teacher, parent or guardian that person hereby takes responsibility that the candidate is entered in accordance with the current syllabus requirements and conditions of entry.
- If you are being taught by an *RGT registered* tutor, please hand this completed form to your tutor and request him/her to administer the entry on your behalf.
- For candidates with special needs, a letter giving details should be attached.

Exam Fee: £__________________ Late Entry Fee (if applicable): £____________________

Total amount submitted: £_________________

Cheques or postal orders should be made payable to University of West London.

Details of conditions of entry, entry deadlines and exam fees are obtainable from the RGT website: www.RGT.org

Once an entry has been accepted, entry fees cannot be refunded.

CANDIDATE INFORMATION (UK Candidates only)

In order to meet our obligations in monitoring the implementation of equal opportunities policies, UK candidates are required to supply the information requested below. The information provided will in no way whatsoever influence the marks awarded during the exam.

Date of birth: ________________ Age: _______ Gender – please circle: male / female

Ethnicity (please enter 2 digit code from chart below): ______ Signed: ____________________

ETHNIC ORIGIN CLASSIFICATIONS (If you prefer not to say, write '17' in the space above.)

White: **01 British** **02 Irish** **03 Other white background**

Mixed: **04 White & black Caribbean** **05 White & black African** **06 White & Asian** **07 Other mixed background**

Asian or Asian British: **08 Indian** **09 Pakistani** **10 Bangladeshi** **11 Other Asian background**

Black or Black British: **12 Caribbean** **13 African** **14 Other black background**

Chinese or Other Ethnic Group: **15 Chinese** **16 Other** **17 Prefer not to say**

I understand and accept the current syllabus regulations and conditions of entry for this exam as specified on the RGT website.

Signed by candidate (if aged 18 or over) ________________________ Date ____________

If candidate is under 18, this form should be signed by a parent/guardian/teacher (circle which applies):

Signed ____________________ Name __________________________ Date _____________

UK ENTRIES

See overleaf for details of how to enter online OR return this form to:

RGT at LCM Examinations, University of West London, St Mary's Road, London W5 5RF

(If you have submitted your entry online do not post this form, instead you need to sign it above and hand it to the examiner on the day of your exam.)

To contact the RGT office telephone 020 8231 2364 or Email office@RGT.org

NON-UK ENTRIES

To locate the address within your country that entry forms should be sent to, and to view exam fees in your currency, visit the RGT website www.RGT.org and navigate to the 'RGT Worldwide' section.